**SOUTH TYNESIDE LIBRARIES
WITHDRAWN FROM STOCK
Date -3. AUG. 1993 Price 30p**

Sold GK

Arthur's
Funny Birthday

Arthur's Funny Birthday

Sophie Davis
Illustrated by Terry Carter

HODDER AND STOUGHTON
LONDON SYDNEY AUCKLAND TORONTO

British Library Cataloguing in Publication Data
Davis, Sophie
  Arthur's funny birthday.
  I. Title   II. Carter, Terry
  823'.9'1J   PZ7.D/

ISBN 0-340-34660-X

Text copyright © 1980 Sophie Davis
Illustrations copyright © 1980 Terry Carter

First published 1980
Second impression 1984

All rights reserved. No part of this publication may be reproduced or transmitted in any form or by any means, electronic or mechanical, including photocopy, recording, or any information storage and retrieval system, without permission in writing from the publisher.

Published by Hodder and Stoughton Children's Books, a division of Hodder and Stoughton Ltd, Mill Road, Dunton Green, Sevenoaks, Kent TN13 2YJ

Printed in Great Britain by St Edmundsbury Press, Bury St Edmunds, Suffolk

Arthur was in a terrible mess.

His damp woollen body lay draped over the edge of the refuse barge. He had lost his socks and his long red legs were trailing in the water behind him.

Floating some way off were a pair of tennis shoes, eight sizes too big, that someone had tied to his feet the night before. Arthur's remaining button eye stared into the bottom of the refuse barge.

If Arthur had been able to think his thought would have run something like this:

'Where am I?'

or,

'What a place to be!'

or,

'Where is it going to end?'

But most important:

'Where did it all begin?'

But Arthur couldn't think. You see Arthur belonged to Nancy and Nancy did all his thinking for him.

It had all begun that morning. Very early that morning.

'Happy birthday,' Nancy had shouted, picking him up from the bottom of her bed. 'You're four today!'

'You're not taking him to school again are you?' asked her brother Ian, putting his head round the door.

''Course I am,' said Nancy, beginning to peel off Arthur's pyjamas. 'He mustn't miss his lessons.'

Ian gave a groan. 'Well – I'm not carrying him again. Not for anything!' he said crossly. Ian, who was older than Nancy, didn't like holding dolls. Particularly Arthur and particularly on the bus.

Arthur's legs always seemed to get in everyone's way.

Only last week part of Arthur's sock had got caught in the conductor's machine. Ian had been carrying Arthur at the time. All the children on the bus had thought it a great joke. All except Ian of course, and the conductor, who wasn't able to

punch out any tickets. The boys in Ian's class hadn't let him forget about it for a whole week.

When Nancy had finished dressing Arthur, Ian came back.

'I mean it,' said Ian. 'If you take him, you carry him all the way and all the way back – the stupid thing!'

'Be quiet,' whispered Nancy, putting her hands over Arthur's ears. 'You'll hurt his feelings.'

'He hasn't got feelings, soppy,' said Ian. 'He isn't a person, you know; he's doll.'

'He *is* a person,' said Nancy, glaring back at her brother. 'He's a woolly person. Granny knitted him and she told me he was real.' But to everyone else Arthur was just a long brown knitted thing with red legs, blue socks and two shoe-button eyes. At night, sitting at the bottom of Nancy's bed, Arthur's eyes would glint in the darkness in a friendly way. His pink mouth was stitched in a permanent smile. You could

say Arthur was a cheerful person – though woolly, of course.

That morning at breakfast Nancy told her mother about the plans for Arthur's birthday.

'After school I'm going to buy him a chocolate cake with four candles.'

'Soppy idiot,' said Ian, crunching his cornflakes.

'Don't tease,' said his mother. 'But does she have to take him to school *every* day?

Everyone laughs at me on the bus!'

But his mother wouldn't listen. She understood why Arthur had to go everywhere with Nancy. It made Nancy feel good and reminded her of home.

Nancy and Ian lived on the nineteenth floor of a tower block, right in the middle of London. They had only lived there a little while and hadn't made any friends yet.

'I wish we'd never moved here,' muttered Ian, while their mother went to fetch their school coats.

Ian stared down far below at the river which threaded its way through the great-coat of the city like a silver ribbon.

'It's a lovely view,' said Nancy, trying to cheer him up.

'You can't ride your bike on a view though, can you?' muttered Ian.

'Dad says we may be able to go back to the old house again one day,' said Nancy sadly. She always felt sad when she remembered their old house.

'What are you two doing staring out of the window?' asked their mother. 'You're going to be late for school.'

The lift arrived with a ping! Nancy, Ian and their mother and, of course Arthur, squeezed inside. There were already lots of people there from the floors above. Crushed together, the lift sped them downwards to the ground floor.

'This lift gives Arthur the collywobbles,' said Nancy clearly. Mother smiled. A boy at the back with red hair started to giggle. He was in Ian's class at school and known as Carrots. Ian pretended not to hear.

'I hope he isn't going to be sick on the bus,' whispered Nancy loudly. The boys at the back of the lift laughed again and nudged one another. 'Look after Nancy now,' said Mother, leaving them at the crowded bus stop. When the bus arrived – a number 36 – it too was very crowded. Arthur's legs dangled as usual amongst all the duffle coats and satchels.

'Two halves to Holmedale School,' said Ian, handing the conductor the money.

'Oh yes, and a quarter for him,' said Nancy loudly, holding Arthur up for the conductor to see. 'He's four today you know.'

'What, dearie?' asked the conductor,

bending over to hear what she was saying.

'Here,' said Nancy, thrusting Arthur into Ian's arms. 'Just hold him till I find the money. I've got five pence somewhere in my satchel.' It was then the giggling began. All the other boys on the bus began to nudge and point at

Ian. Ian turned a funny colour.

'Going to bring Arthur to the match this afternoon?' asked Carrots' friend Frank. Ian pretended not to hear.

'Why have you gone all red?' asked Nancy. 'That boy's talking to you y'know.'

'Perhaps he's got the collywobbles,' giggled Carrots. Ian thrust Arthur back at Nancy, first dropping him on the floor.

'He couldn't even pass the ball,' shouted another.

That morning, Nancy's teacher, Miss Clough, made everyone sit in a large semi-circle on the floor. She told them a long story about Bethlehem and

Christmas. Arthur sat listening, his legs hanging over the side of the 'going home' box. He shared the box today with a panda, a rag doll and a plastic mouse.

From time to time Miss Clough noticed that Nancy clutched at her stomach. 'What's the matter?' she asked later when Nancy refused her milk. 'Nothing much,' said Nancy quietly. 'Just the collywobbles – Arthur's got them too.'

'Oh,' said Miss Clough, looking at Arthur who was smiling as usual.

At lunchtime Nancy couldn't eat her lunch. Staring at her untouched rice pudding, she began to cry.

'Come,' said a voice behind her. 'It

can't taste as bad as all that.' It was Miss Clough. Nancy's tears flowed. She cried softly at first and then louder and louder. Before long she was wrapped up in Miss Clough's coat and lying on the back seat of her Mini. Her stomach was now so painful she even forgot to bring Arthur. He sat waiting patiently in the 'going home' box, smiling.

'But whatever's the matter?' asked Nancy's mother when Miss Clough delivered her to the nineteenth floor.

The Doctor soon came and told them. 'It's her appendix,' he said, writing something down. 'It will have to come out.'

Soon an ambulance came and two nice men wrapped Nancy in a red blanket and took her down in the lift.

'You'll be as right as rice pudding tomorrow,' said the Doctor, with a

smile. But Nancy only made a face. Suddenly she remembered Arthur.

'But what about Arthur? He's got it too you know – the appendix.' But the Doctor didn't seem to be bothered about Arthur.

'I'll bring him up to see you tonight,' whispered Mother, fondly giving her a kiss.

That afternoon, when school came out, Ian couldn't find Nancy. Hundreds of children rushed out of the school gates like a swarm of bees. But Nancy wasn't among them.

Only when the playground had emptied completely except for Ian and the caretaker, did Miss Clough suddenly appear.

'Sorry to keep you, Ian,' she said breathlessly. 'Nancy was taken home at lunchtime. You're to go home and wait for your mother.

'Oh yes – and will you take this home for Nancy?' and without waiting for an answer Miss Clough thrust something at Ian and walked briskly out of the playground. It was Arthur.

On the bus Ian tried to fold Arthur up, but he wouldn't fold. He then tried to sit on him. But it was too uncomfortable. Happily he was almost alone on the bus. Having to wait around for Nancy meant all the other children

had caught earlier buses.

'Ahhhh – 'int he sweet?' said an old lady, tweaking Arthur's nose as she passed. Ian breathed a sigh of relief that Carrots and Frank weren't on the bus. But they were waiting outside the entrance to the block of flats.

As Ian rounded the corner he could see them, tapping a ball to and fro. Ian would have loved to join in. Arthur's long legs dangled down his back. Even if he did get a chance to kick the ball back to one of them, what would they say with this silly woolly toy hung over his shoulder?

Before he could think what he was doing Ian suddenly threw Arthur angrily over a wall he was passing. Behind it he knew was a yard where all the tall rubbish bins of the flats stood waiting to be emptied.

'There,' he said feeling angry. 'I'll be back for you later.' He felt sure Arthur would still be there. Who would want an old knitted doll?

The dog did for a start.

Brian was a wandering red setter who loved long walks and a bit of fun with his exercise. When he saw Arthur come sailing over the wall by the dustbins he pounced at once. After sniffing round Arthur for a minute he picked him up and ran off. Brian loved toys and decided to show Arthur the park. But poor Arthur didn't like the park much.

Brian tended to forget Arthur's long legs which he dragged along in the mud.

A bad-tempered spaniel suddenly dashed up to them. He didn't see much about Arthur that he liked and he began to growl at Brian.

Soon Arthur was being pulled and stretched between the two dogs like a rope in a tug-of-war. Finally Brian got him again and raced away ahead. He bounded up to an old lady who was sitting on a bench.

'Here boy,' said the lady. 'What's this you've got here?' Gently she removed Arthur from Brian's mouth.

Brian sighed and ran off barking. People were always taking away his toys.

'*You're* a funniosity,' said the old lady, examining Arthur. You can go into the jumble sale tomorrow,' she told him, stuffing him into a carrier bag.

When Ian got to his front door that afternoon he found a note stuck to the handle. 'Ian' – it read – 'please call at Number 178.'

Ian stood staring at this for a minute.

Perhaps his mother was out. And where was Nancy?

'Er – ' said a voice behind him, making him jump, 'my mum wants to see you.' Ian turned round and there stood Carrots and Frank. 'She's got a message for you.'

Carrots led the way to his flat. Inside, Ian learnt the news about Nancy. Carrots' mother was very nice and offered him a large slice of cake.

'I – I just have to go downstairs for something,' said Ian. 'Something I dropped.'

Carrots went with him. When they got downstairs Ian clambered quickly over the wall to where he thought he'd thrown Arthur.

'He's gone,' he whispered in dismay when he looked over the top.

'What has?' asked Carrots, climbing up beside him.

'Arthur,' said Ian.

'What was he doing over there?' asked Carrots. Ian didn't like telling lies but he did anyway. 'I – I was just tossing him up and catching him – and over he went.'

Carrots smiled to himself.

'He can't be far away though,' said Ian, dropping over the wall and landing lightly on his feet. 'It was only a minute ago.'

But Arthur was far away. Very far

away. At that moment he was on a 68 bus moving far across London to where Mrs Parkes lived.

Soon he was sitting in Mrs Parkes' hallway, waiting to be collected for a jumble sale the next day. Mrs Parkes had found an old straw boater and put it on his head. It sat there firmly held by a piece of elastic which stretched under Arthur's chin. She also placed a pair of pink plastic sunglasses over his eyes. These she secured by tying some fuse wire round the stems. Warm and dry, Arthur sat beside a rolling pin, some old clothes and three chipped plates.

At exactly half past six there was a knock at the door and some people took Arthur away.

'What a funny old thing,' said one lady, holding Arthur up to the light. 'Where did you find him, Mrs Parkes?'

'The other side of the river dear,' said Mrs Parkes, drinking her tea very fast. 'Being eaten up by a wild animal.'

The lady laughed.

'I've cleaned him up as best I could – even washed his feet! They were filthy,' said Mrs Parkes.

The lady then tucked Arthur under her arm and put him on the back seat of her car.

'Who's he?' asked a voice when the lady started the car up.

'Just a funny doll, dear,' said the lady. 'Why don't you find him a pair of shoes?'

The little girl in the back of the car began to rummage excitedly amongst the heap of jumble in the back of the car. 'I can't find anything to fit,' she said after a while. 'So – I've tied some tennis shoes on him.' And so she had.

It was when they were going over

Westminster Bridge that the car carrying all the jumble suddenly stopped.

'Oh no!' said the lady driving. 'We've run out of petrol!'

'Oh good,' said the little girl holding Arthur. She knew that running out-of-petrol always meant a walk to a garage and she liked that. 'I'll bring him too,' she said, clambering over the piles of jumble, and dragging Arthur with her, his tennis shoes dangling on the ground. When they'd got the can filled, and her mother was busy filling the car, the little

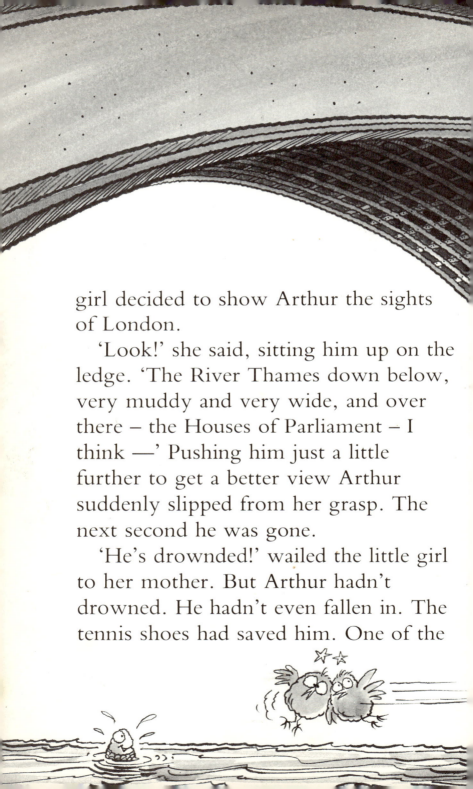

girl decided to show Arthur the sights of London.

'Look!' she said, sitting him up on the ledge. 'The River Thames down below, very muddy and very wide, and over there – the Houses of Parliament – I think —' Pushing him just a little further to get a better view Arthur suddenly slipped from her grasp. The next second he was gone.

'He's drownded!' wailed the little girl to her mother. But Arthur hadn't drowned. He hadn't even fallen in. The tennis shoes had saved him. One of the

laces had caught on a piece of stone that jutted out. You could say he was hanging upside down waiting to fall in. But the little girl and her mother couldn't see him from the top of the bridge and after a while they drove off.

Far below Arthur the river surged and lapped and he could see all sorts of things floating on the water: plastic cups, tin cans and bits of driftwood.

It didn't look like an ideal place to learn how to swim.

Ian and Carrots and Frank looked everywhere for Arthur. They asked in every shop and knocked on almost all the flat doors.

'You couldn't have thrown him into one of the big dustbins when you threw him over, d'you think?' asked Carrots when they got back. 'We never looked there.'

'But if I did – he'll be covered in rubbish by now,' gasped Ian, thinking about Nancy.

'Well – you could always wash him. She'll never notice!' assured Carrots.

'But it'll be dark soon,' said Ian.

'S'all right,' said Carrots, importantly. 'I've got a torch. I'll meet you after I have my tea.'

It was getting dark under Westminster Bridge too. Behind his dark glasses Arthur could just see the barge chugging towards him. It was full of peoples' rubbish and making for the dump at the end of the river.

When it was exactly beneath Arthur the shoelace suddenly snapped, and sent him hurtling downwards. Arthur just missed the water by a hair's-breadth and 'landed on the edge of the barge. There he lay on top of tin cans and potato peelings, looking out at the waterfront as the barge chugged downriver.

When Ian went up on the lift to the nineteenth floor for his tea he felt worried and miserable. He felt even worse when he heard from his father what had happened to Nancy. How could he have thrown away her favourite toy? He felt so bad he couldn't tell his father what had happened.

'Come on, son!' said his father after tea. 'It's all right, you know. An appendix isn't that serious. She'll be home in a week.'

'Home without Arthur,' thought Ian, feeling more and more miserable.

'Oh yes, and don't forget to remind me to take that doll of hers in the morning,' said his father getting up and stretching. 'She'll want it as soon as she

opens her eyes.'

A few minutes later there was a tap at the door. It was Carrots. 'Friend of yours,' said Ian's father, putting his head round the door and smiling.

'Oh,' said Ian. 'Can I go out for a while, Dad?'

'Sure,' said his dad, opening the paper. 'Not too late though. Enjoy yourself!'

If Ian hadn't been so worried about finding Arthur he would have enjoyed himself. Carrots and Frank had both brought torches and were soon inside the huge dustbins poking around with sticks. But the dustbins were very full and very smelly. After throwing the rubbish from one bin to another to try

and empty one of them they decided to give up.

'It's hopeless – we can't even see in the dark,' said Ian.

'We'll just have to get up in the morning very early. Then we can ask the dustbin men to look out for it,' said Carrots, who was very practical. 'It could be right at the bottom!'

'*He*,' said Ian. He never thought he would ever want to see Arthur as much as he did now. That night he lay awake trying to imagine what he would say to Nancy in the morning if he hadn't found Arthur. When he did go to sleep he had a dream that he looked in every dustbin in the City for Arthur.

The funny thing was, Arthur was about to be dropped into the biggest dustbin in the whole of London, the great rubbish tip at the end of the Thames. The barge had stopped

chugging and a huge digger thing with teeth kept dropping down into it and scooping up the refuse. It would then swing over and tip everything out. Arthur, being at the end of the barge, was almost the last thing to be picked up. One of the great teeth caught him by the shoelace and swung Arthur high up into the air. The 'thing' was just about to drop him when suddenly it swung back round towards the barge. It was then the other shoelace snapped, sending Arthur hurtling back down onto the empty barge. He landed with a plonk on

the bow. Half on, half off. The barge started back at once.

Ian woke very early next morning. Carrots had told him the dustbin men came at seven and they had to be there to meet them. Quickly and silently, he slipped into his clothes, hoping he wouldn't wake his father. Downstairs in the yard it was dark and cold and a little bit scary.
'Psssst,' said Carrots, who had

arrived before him. 'I'm over here – they shouldn't be long!'

Over in the hospital Nancy mumbled in her sleep. Her appendix had been taken out and her mother was sleeping beside her.

'Where's Arthur?' she muttered.

'He'll be along very soon, dear,' soothed her mother.

Nancy went back to sleep.

Meanwhile the barge had come all the way back up river. When it arrived at the jetty some dustbin lorries were already waiting to unload from the night before. When they were emptied the dustbin men would take them out on the first collection. 'Ere – look at him!' laughed one of the men standing at the edge of the jetty. He was pointing at Arthur draped over the edge of the

barge. Stooping over, he picked him up and held him up for the other men to see. Arthur looked very odd in his crushed boater and sunglasses.

'You'll do nicely as a mascot,' said the man, taking him over to the lorry. With a piece of rope he'd soon tied Arthur to the front of it.

'We'll call him Albert!' said the driver as they started off for the first collection of the day.

'Here they come,' shouted Carrots, who'd been waiting outside on the road. 'We'll have to be quick before they begin – they work like lightning.'

As soon as the lorry roared up Ian rushed to the first man he could see. 'Hello – er – would you mind having a look for something – I mean before you tip everything away?'

'What kind of "thing"?' asked the man above the roar.

'A toy,' said Ian.

'But what – a car or something?'

'No – it's a doll – Arthur. He's got long legs.'

'Hmmmm,' said the man. 'Well, we'll keep a look out.'

'KEEP A LOOK OUT FOR A DOLL – NAME OF ARFER,' shouted the man to his mates, who all laughed. 'But he might get chewed up,' said Ian anxiously, as he watched the

lorry churning up the refuse.

'If he's there we'll find him,' said the foreman.

But, of course, they didn't. Arthur wasn't in the rubbish lorry, he was *on* it – tied firmly and for all to see – right at the front.

It was Carrots who spotted him. He'd gone round the front of the lorry to take down its number. The men had finished emptying and were all ready to jump back on and leave. The foreman came over to where Ian was standing. 'No,' came a yell from one of the other men.

'Sorry, son,' said the foreman. 'It's just not there.' 'But it *is*,' shouted Carrots, excitedly. 'Ian, quick! Come and have a look!'

Carrots pointed to the front of the dustbin lorry and sure enough there was Arthur, in disguise, of course, but quite

recognisable to anyone who knew him.

'It's Arthur,' said Ian in a whisper.

'Oh – you mean Albert,' said the foreman, untying Arthur and handing him to Ian. 'Talk about luck! Now what was he doing on that barge?'

Ian didn't know the answer to that. He was too relieved to even care. Clutching Arthur tightly to his chest he dashed into the lift with Carrots. Upstairs they did what they could to patch Arthur up. Carrots sewed on a new eye and Ian sponged as much mud away as he could. By the time Ian's father got up he was almost back to normal.

'You're up early, Ian,' said his father putting the kettle on.

'Can I come to the hospital with you?' asked Ian.

'Of course,' said his father.

That morning Ian had no trouble on the bus when he carried Arthur.

'Have you brought him?' was the first thing Nancy said when Ian walked in.

Ian produced Arthur from behind his back. He was still wearing his sunglasses. Ian and Carrots had decided to keep them on to hide the fact that Arthur now had one black eye and one bright blue. Nancy clasped Arthur tightly.

'I like your new glasses,' she whispered in his ear. 'Have you had a boring time without me, Arthur?'

Arthur just smiled and said nothing. Ian became quite fond of Arthur after that.

DM